DATE DUE

the HAMMERHEAD shark

Brad Burnham

The Rosen Publishing Group's
PowerKids Press™
New York

For Omer

Published in 2001 by The Rosen Publishing Group, Inc.
29 East 21st Street, New York, NY 10010
Copyright © 2001 by The Rosen Publishing Group, Inc.

First Edition

Book Design: Maria Melendez

Photo Credits: Cover, title page, pp. 4, 5, 7, 8, 9, 11, 12, 15, 18 © Bettmann/CORBIS; pp. 2, 3,16, 20 © Animals, Animals; pp. 19, 22 © Peter Arnold; pp. 1, 10, 11, 17, 21, 23 © Digital Stock.

Burnham, Brad.
    Hammerhead shark / by Burnham, Brad.
       p. cm.— (The underwater world of sharks)
    Summary: Introduces the physical characteristics, behavior, and habitat of the nine species of hammerhead sharks.
    ISBN 0-8239-5584-2 (alk. paper)
    1. Hammerhead sharks—Juvenile literature. [1. Hammerhead sharks. 2. Sharks.] I. Title. II. Series.

  QL638.95.S7 B87 2000
  597.3'4—dc21   00-024762

Manufactured in the United States of America.

Contents

HAMMERHEADS and FRIENDS

There are nine **species** of hammerhead sharks in the world's oceans. Scientists call the nine types of hammerheads *Sphyrna*, which means hammer in Greek. Some hammerheads have a head shaped like a hammer. Others have a head shaped like the end of a shovel. These are called bonnetheads. The bodies of hammerheads and bonnetheads are like those of other sharks. What makes these sharks unlike any other is that their head is different. The largest hammerhead is the great hammerhead. The largest great hammerhead ever caught was almost 20 feet (6.1 m) long! The smallest hammerhead is the scalloped bonnethead. These sharks grow to 5 feet (1.5 m) long.

◄ You can see how the hammerhead got its name. It really does have a head shaped like a hammer!

There are lots of hammerheads in the oceans. In some parts of the world they are a common kind of shark. They live in the **temperate** and **tropical** regions of the Atlantic and Pacific Oceans. They also live in the Indian Ocean, the Red Sea, and the Mediterranean Sea. Hammerheads are found in areas such as California, Australia, Mexico, Brazil, and New England.

Hammerheads do not always stay in one place. Smooth hammerheads **migrate.** These hammerheads migrate north along the eastern United States in the summer. They travel to the shallow waters between North Carolina and New York. When the water gets cold in the fall, they return to the warmer waters of the Atlantic Ocean.

Hammerheads are found in many parts of the world, including the Mediterranean Sea and the Red Sea. ▶

A FUNNY-LOOKING Head

Hammerhead sharks have oddly shaped heads. Some scientists think that the hammerlike shape makes it easier for the front part of the hammerhead's body to stay afloat.

The shape of their head might also help hammerheads find food. Their eyes, nostrils, and other **sensory organs** are spread out over their wide head. This may help them find their **prey**. Hammerheads might be able to judge distance better than other sharks because their eyes are so far apart.

A hammerhead's strangely shaped head may help it stay afloat. The shape might also help it judge distance and find prey.

9

The **ampullae of Lorenzini** are small tubes located on the **snouts** of all sharks. These small tubes are sensory organs that help sharks feel electricity that is coming from their prey. Hammerhead sharks have a lot of these sensory organs on their wide heads.

All animals produce a little bit of electricity when their muscles move. Hammerheads swim along the bottom of the ocean floor. They move their head back and forth. They do this to pick up the movement from animals that are hiding. This helps the sharks catch their prey.

Hammerheads use sensory organs called ampullae of Lorenzini to track their prey. ▶

School GROUPS

Hammerhead sharks travel in groups called **schools** during the day. The sharks get together in areas like the waters off the coast of Long Island, New York. The schools are made up of mostly females. Each female shark wants to find a male **mate** so she can have babies. There are fewer male than female hammerheads. The females compete for mates. The females try to get a spot in the middle of the school. They do this because they are more likely to be noticed in the middle. Schools of hammerheads swim together all day long. When night comes, the schools break up. The sharks swim off in different directions to find food.

◀ *Hammerheads swim in groups called schools. The schools are usually made up of female sharks looking for mates.*

Eating at NIGHT

Nocturnal animals are animals that are more active at night than during the day. Hammerhead sharks search for food at night. They swim back and forth in areas where their prey might be sleeping.

Stingrays are one type of fish that hammerheads eat. Hammerheads do not seem to mind the stinger that stingrays have on their tail. These stingers get stuck in the mouths of the sharks when they eat them. One hammerhead that was caught by a fisherman had 50 stingers in its mouth. Some stingrays have poison on their stinger. Hammerheads do not seem to be bothered by the poison.

H.C. STORM SCHOOL

Hammerheads hunt for food at night. They eat stingrays, even though some stingrays have poison on their stinger. ▶

Big BRAINS

Hammerhead sharks have brains that are bigger than the brains of most sharks. The biggest parts of their brains are the **olfactory bulbs**.

The olfactory bulbs are responsible for sensing smell. They make up a large part of a hammerhead's brain.

An animal that is wounded and bleeding leaves a trail of odors in the water. Even if the shark cannot see its prey, it can find it by smell. Some sharks can smell a drop of fish blood or fish oil that has been watered down over one million times!

◄ *Hammerheads have bigger brains than most sharks. The brain's olfactory bulbs help hammerheads track their prey by smell.*

Happy BIRTHDAY

Like most sharks, the female hammerhead shark does not lay eggs. She gives birth to babies that have grown inside her. One hammerhead can give birth to between 30 and 40 live babies! Hammerhead babies are called **pups**.

A hammerhead baby gets energy from its mother as it **develops** inside her body. Each baby is attached to the mother by a cord. **Nutrients** travel through the cord from the mother to the baby. The hammerhead is born tail first. The sharks have a better chance of living if the head is protected by the mother's body until it is out of her body. Once the hammerhead babies are born, they are left to take care of themselves.

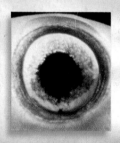

Female hammerheads give birth only once a year. This picture shows a scientist studying a hammerhead pup. ▶

Are HAMMERHEADS DANGEROUS?

In many parts of the world, hammerhead sharks are thought to be dangerous to people. There have been many reports of hammerheads biting people.

In 1805, three large hammerheads were caught off the coast of Long Island, New York. Parts of a human body were found in the stomach of one of the sharks. The shark may have eaten the person after the person was dead. Still, people started to think of hammerheads as man-eaters.

Hammerheads are also dangerous to each other. One 14-foot (4.3-m) hammerhead caught by a fisherman had body parts of four other hammerheads in its stomach. Two of the hammerheads had been swallowed almost whole.

◀ *Hammerheads can be dangerous to people. In 1959, a hammerhead off the coast of California slashed a fisherman's leg.*

HUNTING Hammerheads

Hammerhead sharks are caught for their liver and skin. Oil from the liver is used as a source of vitamin A. The skin is turned into leather and used to make wallets and belts. Hammerheads are also hunted for their fins. When hammerheads began to die out, other kinds of sharks were hunted for fins. There are new laws to stop hunters and fishermen from killing too many sharks. Hopefully, these laws will keep hammerheads and other sharks from becoming **endangered**.

Glossary

ampullae of Lorenzini (am-pyool-AY UV lor-en-ZEE-nee) Small tubes on the snouts of sharks that can sense electricity.

develops (dih-VEH-lups) Grows.

endangered (en-DAYN-jerd) When something is in danger of no longer existing.

mate (MAYT) Either of a pair of animals that join together to make babies.

migrate (MY-grayt) When large groups of animals or people move from one place to another.

nocturnal (nok-TER-nul) To be active during the night.

nutrients (NOO-tree-ints) What a living thing needs for energy or to grow.

olfactory bulbs (ol-FAK-teh-ree BULBZ) The part of the brain that senses smell.

prey (PRAY) An animal that is eaten by another animal for food.

pups (PUPS) A type of baby animal.

schools (SKOOLZ) Groups of fish.

sensory organs (SEN-suh-ree OR-genz) Groups of cells that help an animal understand its surroundings.

snouts (SNOWTS) Part of animal heads that include the nose, mouth, and jaw.

species (SPEE-sheez) A group of living things that have certain basic things in common.

Sphyrna (SFEER-na) The scientific name for hammerhead sharks.

temperate (TEM-puh-rit) An area that is neither too hot nor too cold.

tropical (TRAH-pih-kul) An area that is very hot and humid year round.

Index

B
babies, 13, 18
bodies, 5, 9, 18, 21
brains, 17

E
eyes, 9

F
fins, 22
food, 9, 13, 14

H
head, 5, 9, 10, 18

L
liver, 22

M
migrate, 6
mouths, 14

N
nostrils, 9

O
olfactory bulbs, 17

P
prey, 9, 10, 14, 17

S
schools, 13
sensory organs, 9, 10
skin, 22
smell, 17
snouts, 10
swim, 10, 13, 14

T
tail, 18

Web Sites

To find out more about hammerhead sharks, check out these Web sites:

http://www.EnchantedLearning.com/subjects/sharks/species/Hammerhead.shtml

http://www.sdnhm.org/kids/sharks/shore-to-sea/hammerhead.html